Our Branch in Brussels

A Play

David Campton

A SAMUEL FRENCH ACTING EDITION

SAMUEL FRENCH

FOUNDED 1830

SAMUELFRENCH-LONDON.CO.UK
SAMUELFRENCH.COM

CHARACTERS

Mrs Jane Bee
Effie
Daisy
Miss Felicia Laurelle
Mrs Maud Hardie
Miss Beatrice Endicott

Time—the second half of the Nineteenth Century

OUR BRANCH IN BRUSSELS*

The first floor drawing-room of Mrs Bee's house

Taste in furnishing has taken precedence over money, though there is no shortage of either. Upstage R is a fireplace with a vase of flowers standing inside. Below the fireplace stands a cabinet containing an assortment of bottles, decanters and glasses. L is a large window with a desk and chair in front. A chair stands either side of the window. Upstage L is a door leading to the landing and stairs (or an arch with the door off). In the middle of the room, slightly L of the centre is a couch with a low table at the head and a screen behind

As the CURTAIN *rises Mrs Bee is setting out papers, ledgers etc. on her desk. Although no longer in the first flush of youth, elegance combines with assurance to produce an effect of time-defying vitality—an effect enhanced by cunningly-engineered undergarments and the most subtle touches to her complexion. She pauses and surveys the room. Effie, her parlour-maid, waits for instructions*

Mrs Bee Tea is in hand, I presume?

Effie Kettle's on the boil, ma'am.

Mrs Bee The strongest brew for this committee, Effie. Pointless to waste Lapsong on palates debilitated by Church Room tea urns. The ladies are due now. Show them up as and when they arrive.

Effie What about other visitors, ma'am?

Mrs Bee We are not at home. This afternoon is devoted to The Bountiful Bequest.

Effie There is a young person, ma'am ...

Mrs Bee What about her?

Effie Waiting, ma'am. First on one side of the street and then on the other. Wanting to take the plunge, you might say, but daring herself to climb the front steps.

Mrs Bee (*turning to the window*) You've developed a knowing eye, Effie.

Effie Experience, ma'am.

Mrs Bee (*looking down*) Respectable?

---

*N.B. Paragraph 3 on page ii of this Acting Edition regarding photocopying and video-recording should be carefully read.

Effie On the outside, ma'am. You'll need time to find out about other sides. But with ladies expected ...

Mrs Bee There has been a falling-off in their charitable enthusiasm lately. What better spur than a demonstration of the need for it? If the girl should be an unfortunate ... Ah! (*She bows slightly with aristocratic condescension*)

Effie She spotted you, ma'am?

Mrs Bee Show her up.

Effie She hasn't rung yet, ma'am.

Mrs Bee She will now. ... The regular routine, Effie.

Effie I don't know why you bother, ma'am.

Mrs Bee Goats must be sorted from sheep.

Effie In the long run they all go the same way.

Mrs Bee But by different routes.

The doorbell rings

Mrs Bee You should be at the door.

Effie Yes, ma'am.

Effie exits

Mrs Bee unlocks the cabinet and puts a decanter and glass on the table by the couch, adding a few drops to the bottom of the glass from a smaller bottle. She opens a box of confectionery, which she has also taken from the cabinet, and places it on the table, leaving the lid slightly askew to reveal its contents. She then opens her purse, and spilling a few coins onto the desk, leaves it beside them. Mrs Bee crosses to the door and hears distant voices from below. Realizing that the screen is not where it should be, she makes a gesture of impatience, then pulls it to the far corner of the room. She just has time to slip out of sight as:

Effie and Daisy enter

A person, ma'am, who declines to state her business on the doorstep. ... (*She looks around the room*) Oh. (*Slightly unconvincingly as though delivering a speech learned by rote*) The mistress must have slipped out for a moment. I am sure she will not be long. If you do not object to being left alone ...

Daisy (*casually*) Please yourself.

Effie But do not go touching nothing. Some of them knick-knacks is very valuable. In fact, the smaller they are the more valuable they come.

Daisy (*without interest*) Is that a fact?

Effie I should not wish to find myself paying for somebody else's breakages.

Daisy You won't.

Effie As long as you understand.

Daisy I understand all right.

Effie Right, then.

Effie exits closing the door behind her

Daisy goes to the fireplace, nonchalantly swinging her reticule. She picks up a figurine from the shelf, looks at it and puts it back. Then she turns and surveys the rest of the room. She goes to the table, unstoppers the decanter, sniffs, then puts it back. With one finger she flicks open the lid of the sweet box and glances at its contents. With a growing smile she crosses to the desk and examines the purse, but with hands behind her back, taking nothing. She faces the room again, addressing apparently empty air

Daisy What now, lady? Will you creep in, soft-like? Or will you pounce like something out of a pantomime?

Mrs Bee (*emerging from behind the screen*) My entrances are never like something out of a pantomime, nor do I creep. I am glad our little test ended satisfactorily; but you'll realize——

Daisy What you was up to? Tempting a young innocent? Naughty. Mind you, I was never young enough to be that innocent.

Mrs Bee Don't you care for sugared almonds?

Daisy I'm after more than sweets.

Mrs Bee Then we must do what we can for you. (*She crosses to her desk*)

Daisy You do that.

Mrs Bee moves a chair from against the wall to a position facing the desk

Mrs Bee Be seated.

Daisy If you say so. (*Rather suspiciously, she sits*)

Mrs Bee How did you hear of us?

Daisy The usual way—keeping my ears open.

Mrs Bee The object of this charity is the relief of distressed females.

Daisy Well, I'm female and distressed.

Mrs Bee (*sitting behind the desk*) Tell me more. Names—correct if possible. Address—if any. Employment—if appropriate. Relations—if known. Generosity must be tempered with caution. A few routine questions——

Daisy I'll ask the questions.

Mrs Bee I don't much care for that attitude.

Daisy Take it or leave it.

Mrs Bee In which case proceeding further would be a waste of time.

Daisy Don't you believe it.

Mrs Bee You are not a young female to strike our Committee as a deserving cause. You might even prejudice them against causes to come.

Daisy What about the causes that 'ave gone? My friends, like.

Mrs Bee If your friends are anything like you, I am happy to say we are unacquainted.

Daisy Bella, now.

Mrs Bee Bella—who?

Daisy Pretty little thing—Bella. Once you scraped off the top layer of muck. Are you in charge of handing out the soap?

Mrs Bee Did this Bella tell you of us?

Daisy Not in so many words. Nods and winks more like. Told me she'd found a soft touch—a place to go when you're up against it. Wouldn't give no names—secretive little cat. But she lent me half a crown. Then, all of a sudden, she was gone. Was that natural—with me still owin' her half a crown? Then one day I was sittin' on our front steps and thinkin'—mainly about where my next dinner was comin' from—when in front of me stands an old biddy with a can o' soup in one hand, a bar o' soap in the other and chunterin' on about cleanliness bein' next to godliness.

Mrs Bee *Old* biddy?

Daisy "In trouble?" she asked. "Remember this address." Actually I didn't. Not at once. The soup was fillin' all right, but it was the soap what made all the difference. It worked so well on my hands and face I tried it all over. That's when men started payin' for my drinks. ... Took my mind right off Bella for a while. In fact it was only after Maisie and Tilly and Cissie that I began to put two and two together. I can add up. Them girls was all pretty. Even prettier after the soup an' soap 'ad filled 'em out and cleaned 'em up.

Mrs Bee Are you connecting me with that process?
Daisy I can't recollect the word for what you do, lady—but I'll lay a hundred to one it's against the law.
Mrs Bee What do you want?
Daisy Want? I want. . . . What do I want? Haven't got around to thinkin' overmuch about that. Just give me a minute.

The clock strikes three

Mrs Bee I don't have a minute to spare. You can't sit thinking there all afternoon.
Daisy Expectin' somebody else?
Mrs Bee Let us agree a price.
Daisy That's a smartish about turn.
Mrs Bee We'll drink to a speedy settlement. (*She crosses to the table*)
Daisy You're not gettin' rid of me that easy.
Mrs Bee Getting rid?
Daisy I'm a clinger, I am.
Mrs Bee (*picking up the decanter*) Gin? (*She pours out into the waiting glass*)
Daisy (*sarcastically*) It has to be gin for my sort, of course. Especially at three o'clock in the afternoon. Do 'ave a noggin' o' mother's ruin with your cucumber sandwiches, Daisy, dear.
Mrs Bee There are no cucumber sandwiches, Daisy, dear. And you may select your own road to ruin. (*She opens the cabinet door*) Brandy, rum, whisky, port, sherry, curaçao, cointreau, kummel . . .
Daisy What's a lady like you doin' with that barful?
Mrs Bee I try to be prepared for any emergency.
Daisy I've never tried kummel before.
Mrs Bee Kummel it shall be. This glass is small, because a little goes a long way. (*She pours a drink into a liqueur glass*)
Daisy Far cry from soup.
Mrs Bee *You* have come a long way since then, my dear. And I expect you to go further.

Mrs Bee, with her back turned to hide from Daisy what she is doing, adds a few drops from the small bottle. Even if Daisy cannot see what is happening she has suspicions

Daisy What do you mean by that?
Mrs Bee No more than you suppose I mean. (*She hands over the*

glass) Flavoured with carraway. Perhaps a suitable accompaniment to seed cake. But you will not be our guest at tea.
Daisy We haven't come to terms yet.
Mrs Bee We shall, my dear. Drink up.

Daisy puts the glass on the desk

Daisy Really, you're too good to be true.
Mrs Bee You haven't tasted it.
Daisy I know what they put in babies' daffys to keep 'em quiet.
Mrs Bee Surely you don't suspect me of lacing good liqueur with laudenum.
Daisy I wouldn't expect a lady like you to have heard of laudenum. (*She picks up the glass again, but does not drink*)
Mrs Bee I think you'll be more comfortable on the couch. Be careful not to spill your kummel.
Daisy Don't you mean—down it quick? (*With exaggerated caution she crosses to the couch, puts the glass on the table, then sits*) Not a drop spilt.
Mrs Bee Unnecessary precaution.
Daisy You're not drinkin'.
Mrs Bee There is one cordial I reserve for very special occasions. Now—where ... ?

Mrs Bee takes a small blue bottle from the cabinet and with head slightly averted unstoppers it. As Daisy chatters on she moves behind the couch, picks up a small cushion, and sprinkles some of the contents from the bottle on to it

Daisy There's a lot of wickedness in the world, lady. You wouldn't believe.
Mrs Bee Wouldn't I?
Daisy I've heard of girls takin' drinks from strangers and wakin' up in places where they couldn't write home to mother.
Mrs Bee Fascinating.
Daisy Now, if you was to drink half this, I might be tempted to risk the other half.
Mrs Bee That won't be necessary.
Daisy I'm not wakin' up in no fancy place off Piccadilly.
Mrs Bee Of course not, my dear. Much further off than that.

Mrs Bee pushes the cushion over Daisy's face. Daisy struggles, but, with Mrs Bee behind her, is at a disadvantage

So sorry, Daisy. But we can't have our little wild flowers popping up in the wrong beds, can we? Nice deep breaths, dear.

The doorbell rings

And please don't take too long about it. We have visitors.

Daisy suddenly goes limp

My goodness, that was quick. This is the first occasion I have had to use chloroform. Others accepted their gin without argument. (*She removes the cushion*) Off like a baby. Almost a pity to disturb you, but you could prove an embarrassment where you are. You'll sleep just as soundly in the corner. Ups-a-daisy.

Mrs Bee heaves Daisy off of the couch and drags her behind the screen

(*Unseen*) Just time, I trust, to dispose of the evidence . . .

Effie enters ushering in Miss Laurelle, a wistful person of uncertain age and whose life has so far lacked much point, and Mrs Hardie, a widow who has turned to good works as a substitute for a husband

Effie Miss Laurelle, ma'am . . .
Miss Laurelle Dear Jane . . . (*she looks around the apparently empty room*) Oh.
Effie And Mrs Hardie.
Mrs Hardie Jane not here?
Effie She was.
Mrs Hardie Then where?
Mrs Bee (*unseen*) Not a million miles away.

Mrs Bee emerges from behind the screen and carefully adjusts it to hide what is behind

Miss Laurelle Dear Jane.
Mrs Bee Dear Felicia. Dear Maud. Tea, Effie. Tea.
Effie Directly, ma'am.

Effie exits

Mrs Bee You are visibly wilting, dears. Make yourselves at ease.

Mrs Bee just has time to snatch the small cushion from behind Miss

Laurelle as she sits on the couch. Mrs Hardie sniffs loudly. Mrs Bee realizes that she can smell chloroform

Mrs Bee You are here before dear Henrietta or dear Beatrice.

Miss Laurelle Dear Henrietta sends her apologies. Her Mothers' Union is facing another crisis.

Mrs Bee Too many mothers and not enough union?

Mrs Hardie sniffs again. Mrs Bee tosses the cushion over the screen

Hay fever or summer cold, dear Maud?

Mrs Hardie (*sniffing*) What can I smell?

Mrs Bee The flowers, maybe. Such a heavy perfume. Does it put you in mind of oriental gardens?

Mrs Hardie (*sitting next to Miss Laurelle*) It puts me in mind of a hospital.

Miss Laurelle Ah, but you are better acquainted with hospitals than with oriental gardens, dear Maud. (*She wriggles uncomfortably*) So many ... good works. ... I ... appear ... to be ...

Mrs Hardie Ill at ease, dear?

Miss Laurelle pulls from under her Daisy's reticule, left on the couch

Miss Laurelle This would appear to be ...

Mrs Hardie A reticule.

Miss Laurelle It appears to have been ...

Mrs Hardie Sat upon.

Mrs Bee (*hastily repossessing the bag*) Idiot girl!

Miss Laurelle I do apologize, dear Jane. I hadn't expected to find a reticule where it might be sat upon.

Mrs Bee Not you, dear Felicia. A previous visitor. An applicant for aid. Indisposed.

Mrs Hardie Without warning?

Mrs Bee Warnings would have been wasted on that one. I did what had to be done.

Mrs Hardie Smelling salts?

Mrs Bee Of a sort. (*She puts the reticule on the desk next to the glass of gin*)

Miss Laurelle (*pointing to the gin*) Sal volatile?

Mrs Bee Ah. You noticed.

Miss Laurelle So right for a fainting fit. A few drops in water.

Mrs Bee My entire medicine chest was at her disposal.

Miss Laurelle Dear Jane! So prompt to help.

Mrs Bee (*sniffing at the gin*) Perhaps this is what you could smell, dear Maud. Most pungent. (*She replaces the glass in a less conspicuous position*)

Mrs Hardie (*indicating the kummel glass on the table*) What about . . .?

Mrs Bee A—herbal remedy. In case other treatment failed.

Mrs Hardie Herbal, eh? Interesting. May I taste?

Mrs Hardie stretches out a hand for the glass but Mrs Bee gets to it first

Mrs Bee (*taking the glass to the desk*) Better not.

There is a knock at the door

You wouldn't want to spoil your tea.

Effie enters with a tray of tea-things

On the desk, Effie.

Effie Seed cake today, ma'am.

Mrs Bee Thank you, Effie.

Effie puts down the tray and exits

Dear Beatrice is going to be late.

Mrs Hardie Didn't I pass on the message? Talk of hospitals must have put it out of my mind. She'll be calling on the Bishop's Chaplain first—a question of confirmation or embrocation. She wants us to start without her. Says we shan't have decided anything and she can catch up on our blather in a couple of minutes. You know the way she talks.

Mrs Bee So like dear Beatrice. Then we can take her advice and our tea at the same time. (*She busies herself with the tea as she talks*) Outlining our financial difficulties——

Miss Laurelle Not figures again, dear Jane.

Mrs Bee Even beef bones and lentils must be bought and paid for. And soup is only part of our benefactions. Recent assistance has included boots, blankets, firewood, paregoric and a wooden leg.

Mrs Hardie Wasn't a wooden leg somewhat extravagant?

Mrs Bee Not to a person with no other means of support. It has always been our boast that no deserving cause is turned away. And the claims on us increase.

Miss Laurelle If only the poor could be persuaded not to proliferate.

Mrs Bee That is their problem, Felicia, dear. Meanwhile we have a crisis of our own to surmount.

Mrs Hardie Did you say seed cake?

Mrs Bee I said seed cake. I mean debts.

Miss Laurelle You are so resourceful, Jane dear. Where did all the other money come from?

Daisy (*emerging from behind the screen*) That's what I'd like to know.

Mrs Hardie Where did you come from?

Mrs Bee (*calmly*) Tea, Maude? And a slice of seed cake? (*She hands over a cup, saucer and plate to Mrs Hardie*)

Daisy What's more, I want to know the rest. What's more I'm not leaving 'till I do. What's more, when I do——

Mrs Bee Tea, Felicia, dear?

Miss Laurelle Who is this?

Mrs Bee Will you take tea, Daisy, dear?

Daisy Don't you Daisy me. After doing what you tried to do. Tea! Is that what you did to all the others?

Mrs Bee Never in tea, dear. Some things are sacred. (*She pours out another cupful*)

Mrs Hardie Others?

Mrs Bee A mistake. A little learning can be so dangerous.

Daisy I held my breath.

Mrs Bee I should have suspected oblivion came too promptly. But I am no expert in administering anaesthetics.

Miss Laurelle Is she sitting on our committee?

Daisy I'm not sitting anywhere here.

Mrs Bee You'll manage your cup and saucer more easily if you do. Try the couch between the ladies.

Daisy I've had enough of that couch. And you're no ladies. None of you—doing what you do to defenceless girls.

Miss Laurelle Doing what?

Daisy Doing away with them.

Mrs Hardie Don't maunder, girl.

Miss Laurelle We have never done away with anyone. Have we?

Mrs Bee Not knowingly.

Mrs Hardie Don't hover, girl. Sit.

Daisy Well . . .

Daisy's attention is distracted as she sits down. Mrs Bee takes

*advantage of this to empty the contents of the gin glass into her cup
of tea*

I ought to have my head examined—knowing what I know.

Mrs Bee Tea. Hot, sweet and strong. (*She hands over a cup of tea
to Daisy*)

Daisy I shouldn't. Only after going through what I've just been
through a girl needs a drop of something. And, like you say, tea
ought to be safe. Especially when everybody else is drinking it.
(*She glares at the other two ladies*)

*Miss Laurelle and Mrs Hardie sip their tea uncertainly. Daisy is
about to, but changes her mind*

You *are* drinking, aren't you?

Mrs Bee I am about to. (*She pours out a cup of tea*)

Daisy (*sips*) Hot. (*She tips some into her saucer, blows on it, and
drinks*) And strong.

Mrs Bee My special blend.

Miss Laurelle Dear Jane prides herself on her brew.

Mrs Hardie You've never had tea like this before.

Mrs Bee Nor will again. (*She drinks*)

Daisy (*after emptying her cup*) If there was more tea like this,
there'd be less call for gin.

Mrs Hardie Stick to tea, dear.

Miss Laurelle A girl can't go far wrong if she avoids strong drink.

Mrs Hardie And temptation.

Daisy Do you Greenlanders know what goes on here?

Mrs Hardie We are The Committee.

Miss Laurelle Not forgetting dear Henrietta and dear Beatrice—
but they have other interests.

Mrs Hardie We, on the other hand, are totally devoted to The
Bequest.

Miss Laurelle With Mrs Bee at the helm—to employ a nautical
term.

Daisy (*with slightly slurred speech*) Oh, if we're being shipmates—
do you know what cargo you carry? Shall you tell 'em, Captain,
or shall I?

Mrs Bee You're sure you won't have any seed cake?

Daisy What's in it?

Mrs Bee Seeds.

Daisy Why do you want me to have seed cake?
Mrs Bee Because you can't talk with your mouth full.
Daisy Oh, can't I?
Miss Laurelle To pursue the maritime metaphor, I am all at sea.
Daisy Watch out for storms. ... Seeds?
Mrs Bee Carraway. Have you finished with that cup? (*She rescues it from Daisy*)
Daisy Like in kummel?
Mrs Bee Exactly as in kummel.
Daisy (*smugly*) I didn't drink the kummel.
Mrs Bee You drank the tea.
Daisy But you said—never in tea.
Mrs Bee There's a first time for everything.
Daisy But this pair aren't. ... They didn't ... (*She yawns*)
Mrs Bee Not *their* tea, dear. Yours.
Daisy (*struggling to her feet*) You can't——
Mrs Bee I fear I had to. We can't allow you to whistle up a wind, can we?
Mrs Hardie (*having difficulty in holding on to her cup, saucer and plate*) Do sit still, girl.
Daisy (*now having difficulty in focusing*) Listen to me, you two. You're in this with her.
Miss Laurelle In what?
Daisy Ask her.
Mrs Hardie Ask what?
Daisy (*staggering*) Ask ... where the money comes from. Ask ... where the girls go to. Ask ... what she put in my. ... Just ask. ... anything. Oooooh. ... (*In the middle of a yawn she sinks to the floor and goes to sleep*)
Miss Laurelle My dear. ... Oh, dear. ... Jane, dear ...
Mrs Bee A lesson in discretion.
Miss Laurelle What did she mean by asking?
Mrs Bee What I mean by discretion.
Miss Laurelle What money? What girls?
Mrs Bee I'm sure you'd rather not know.
Mrs Hardie She said something about—tea.
Mrs Bee I hoped she might have—dropped off a little sooner. Before she had time to "blow the gaff" as our sailors say.
Mrs Hardie You must deny such a monstrous accusation.
Mrs Bee How can I? With this one asleep in the deep.
Mrs Hardie But how? What?

Mrs Bee Laudenum, dear. Obtainable from any reliable pharmacy. Ideal for disposing of toothache, sea-sickness—or other nuisances. However this one can't be left where she is.

Mrs Hardie Why? Why?

Mrs Bee Because dear Beatrice is expected at any moment.

Mrs Hardie Why laudenum?

Mrs Bee The silly creature was demanding money with menaces. Will you help me to move her? I'll relieve you of your cup and saucer. (*She takes them from Mrs Hardie and puts them on the desk*)

Mrs Hardie No, dear.

Mrs Bee That's most uncooperative, dear. Felicia, then. (*She takes Miss Laurelle's cup and saucer and puts them on the desk*)

Mrs Hardie Don't stir.

Miss Laurelle I don't believe I could. Should we put a cushion under her head?

Mrs Bee She won't notice—for several hours.

Miss Laurelle How do you know? Oh!

Mrs Hardie An explanation is called for, dear Jane.

Mrs Bee There's hardly time, dear Maud. Sooner or later Beatrice will tear herself from the dear Bishop's Chaplain. Some things could never be explained to dear Beatrice. She is very set in her ways.

Mrs Hardie You haven't explained to us.

Mrs Bee What you don't know can't harm you.

Mrs Hardie I insist. Felicia?

Miss Laurelle (*feebly*) We insist.

Mrs Bee Do you understand what you are doing?

Mrs Hardie We are trying to understand what *you* are doing. The truth, if you please.

Mrs Bee Very well. There's no time, anyway, to invent a convincing lie. ... The Bountiful Bequest has a branch in Brussels.

Mrs Hardie I wasn't aware of that.

Mrs Bee Why should you be? The accounts are kept quite separate. The profits are transferred to our balance sheet as anonymous benefactions.

Mrs Hardie You mean money donated in Brussels is distributed here.

Mrs Bee I'm so glad you understand. Now that little difficulty has been disposed of, can we do likewise with the one sleeping on the rug?

Mrs Hardie Her!

Mrs Bee She should be on her way. Could we carry her down between us?

Mrs Hardie (*horrified*) No!

Mrs Bee You may be right. We could meet Beatrice on the way up. So unlucky to pass on the stairs, I'm told.

Mrs Hardie On her way—to where?

Mrs Bee To our branch in Brussels, of course. To join the others—on active service.

Mrs Hardie On? You mean our branch in Brussels is . . . ?

Mrs Bee Shush, dear. Such an inelegant word. Sounds like a soup kitchen. Just say that Our Charity is funded from The Continent.

Miss Laurelle gives a high-pitched screech

Indisposition, dear, or an opinion?

Miss Laurelle continues to let off steam in a series of shrill hoots

Mrs Hardie I feel the same, Felicia, but am *I* giving way? Can't we administer something? (*Her eye falls ·on the glass of kummel*) Here.

Mrs Hardie is about to pass the glass to Miss Laurelle when Mrs Bee intercepts it

Mrs Bee No! Not that!

Mrs Hardie Would it not calm her?

Mrs Bee Too well. (*She puts down the glass on the tea tray, then shakes Miss Laurelle*) Hush, dear. Hush, I say. Hush.

Miss Laurelle's shrieks subside

That's better. Why this exhibition of outraged virtue?

Mrs Hardie How can you ask? Those poor girls. What about *their* virtue?

Mrs Bee I doubt if the word holds quite the same meaning for them. We are merely putting a natural propensity to profitable purposes.

Mrs Hardie We? You mean—us?

Mrs Bee Dear Maud. Dear Felicia. You are both on the board of trustees.

Mrs Hardie These doubtful activities must cease at once.

Mrs Bee Are you putting a proposal before this committee? Is it seconded?

Miss Laurelle (*hiccoughing*) Ay.

Mrs Bee You wish to wind up The Charity?

Mrs Hardie I did not say that.

Mrs Bee It amounts to the same thing. No more boots or blankets. No more paregoric or wooden legs. Because without the wherewith all our largesse must come to a full stop. Shall we take a vote now? Two to one against, I believe.

Mrs Hardie Let us—not be hasty.

Miss Laurelle Maud!

Mrs Hardie We cannot countenance immorality . . .

Miss Laurelle Never!

Mrs Hardie Yet, condoned or not, it will persist.

Mrs Bee Admirably expressed, Maud.

Miss Laurelle Could you sleep comfortably with those crimes on your conscience?

Mrs Bee On the other hand, will your sleeping conscience keep the poor of this parish from want?

Miss Laurelle But such a price . . .

Mrs Bee A few sleepless nights on behalf of our dependants? Put that to your conscience.

Miss Laurelle My conscience is not so easily stretched.

Mrs Bee How do you know, dear? Have you exercised it much recently?

Mrs Hardie Think, dear Felicia . . .

Miss Laurelle I am thinking—of those girls in Brussels.

Mrs Bee More to the point, think of this one here.

The doorbell rings

Mrs Hardie The bell! Beatrice?

Mrs Bee Who else? It's now or never, Felicia—with a mere twenty-six stairs between Beatrice and that door. You may have second thoughts . . .

Miss Laurelle I shall not.

Mrs Bee But our dear Beatrice is less likely to be swayed than Nelson's column.

Miss Laurelle In which case I shall be relieved of all responsibility.

Mrs Bee If this exhibit is still on display when that door opens, a great many grannies will face a cold and hungry winter. . . . Now—will you help stow her behind that screen?

Miss Laurelle Can't you lift her without me? You must have done so before.

Mrs Bee Why should Maud and I waste our efforts if you tell Beatrice to peek.

Miss Laurelle Oh, I'd never do that.

Mrs Bee No?

Miss Laurelle That would be sneaking.

Mrs Bee Then you are with us.

Miss Laurelle I didn't say so.

Mrs Hardie Actions speak louder, dear Felicia. Lend a hand.

Miss Laurelle (*reluctantly*) How—is she to be conveyed?

Mrs Bee I'll raise her to a sitting position. (*She sits Daisy up*) Then, Maud, if we place one arm round your neck—you'll need to bend—and one arm round yours, Felicia . . .

Miss Laurelle Round mine?

Mrs Bee Only twenty-six steps dear, and Beatrice is climbing them now.

Miss Laurelle Oh—very well.

Miss Laurelle and Mrs Hardie bend and drape Daisy's arms round their shoulders

Mrs Bee Hold tightly to her arms, then straighten up.

Miss Laurelle and Mrs Hardie, with assistance from Mrs Bee, straighten Daisy up and end up by supporting her between them

That wasn't so difficult after all, dears. I knew you could take the strain—conscience and all.

Miss Laurelle What now?

Mrs Hardie Behind the screen?

Effie enters

Mrs Bee No time.

Effie Miss Endicott, ma'am.

Mrs Bee To the couch. (*She sweeps to the door*) My dear Beatrice . . .

Miss Laurelle and Mrs Hardie take two steps back and flop onto the couch, propping up Daisy between them

Miss Endicott enters, puffing. She is a grim, grey, short-sighted person. She carries a black cane, which she uses for emphasis more than support

Miss Endicott (*brusquely*) Jane.

Mrs Bee directs Miss Endicott to the chair below the desk, keeping herself between the newcomer and the trio on the couch

Mrs Bee How did you find the dear Bishop's Chaplain?
Miss Endicott As pusillanimous as ever. After five minutes of his oozing I feel like laying about him. (*She relieves some of her frustration by giving the chair seat in front of her a hearty whack with her cane*) But the squelchy little toad would probably enjoy it. (*She sits*)

Meanwhile Mrs Hardie is packing cushions behind Daisy to keep her in an upright position

Miss Endicott nods brusque greetings in their direction

Miss Endicott Maud, Felicia, Henrietta . . .

Each lady nods in turn, Mrs Hardie manipulates Daisy's head for her

(*pointing short-sightedly with the cane*) Henrietta?
Mrs Hardie Daisy. She is . . . er . . .
Mrs Bee Representing our beneficiaries.
Mrs Hardie Yes. Representing.
Miss Endicott How de do?

Mrs Hardie manipulates Daisy's arm in a gesture of salutation

Mrs Bee Tea, Beatrice? Seed cake?
Miss Endicott No time to waste this afternoon. Wasted enough already. Why won't people move without prodding? I blame modern education. So much beating in schools today that nothing gets done without threatening corporal punishment. I believe some actually become addicted to the cane. Hard now to tell what counts as stick and what as carrot. . . . Seed cake? I can cope with a slice at the same time as the accounts.
Effie Fresh tea, ma'am?
Miss Endicott Don't offer me your straw-coloured puddle-waste. If it's been standing it may be the right colour for once.
Mrs Bee Take a message, Effie. To Jim, the carter's lad.
Effie Now, ma'am?
Mrs Bee Urgent. Baggage for Brussels.
Effie Yes, ma'am.

Effie exits

Miss Laurelle Does she—understand?
Mrs Bee We understand each other.
Miss Endicott This business of the deficit . . .
Mrs Bee An increase in income is imminent. Yes, Daisy?

Mrs Hardie organizes another wave from Daisy

Miss Endicott Mere speculation. Face facts. I hope the ledger has
   been properly kept.
Mrs Bee Every item of income and expenditure.
Miss Endicott When money flows out faster than it flows in
   suspect the incidental expenses. The ledger, please.
Mrs Bee And a slice of seed cake. (*She hands the ledger and a slice
   of seed cake to Miss Endicott*)
Miss Endicott Stop the drain.
Mrs Bee We are not plumbers, Beatrice, dear.
Miss Endicott Few of you philanthropists appreciate money. Let
   it run to waste. (*She eats the seed cake as she examines the ledger*)
Mrs Hardie The purpose of this organization is to render assist-
   ance.
Miss Endicott What's this? Spirits!
Miss Laurelle Do they need assistance?
Miss Endicott Gin, brandy, rum and—is this kummel?
Mrs Bee Kummel.
Miss Endicott Is kummel necessary?
Mrs Bee Sometimes very.
Miss Endicott Soup is a necessity—strong drink is an extrava-
   gance. We serve soup.
Mrs Bee Soup will not always serve.
Miss Endicott I disapprove of stimulants. . . . Didn't you mention
   tea? And there's too much seed in this cake. More extravagance.
Mrs Bee Lend me your cane and I'll chastise the pastrycook.
Miss Endicott Flippancy! This situation is serious. (*She turns more
   pages then gives a hoot*) Ah!
Miss Laurelle (*jumping*) Oh!

*Miss Laurelle's sudden start causes Daisy to slide over. Hastily Miss
Laurelle pushes Daisy back into place*

Miss Endicott Did you say who? Why, you.
Miss Laurelle Me?

Miss Endicott All of you. Look at this.
Mrs Bee Tea, Beatrice. (*She passes a cup to Miss Endicott*)
Miss Endicott This carriage.
Mrs Hardie Whose carriage?
Mrs Bee You mean the carter's charges.
Miss Endicott Exorbitant.
Mrs Bee They may be somewhat above normal——
Miss Endicott Normal? I could cross to Calais for less.
Mrs Bee The fare to Ostend is higher and the goods are perishable.
Miss Endicott What goods?
Miss Laurelle (*with a little wail*) Ooooh!
Miss Endicott Yes?
Mrs Bee They need to be handled with care.
Miss Endicott And . . . and here's ten shillings for laudenum.
Mrs Bee You consider that price unreasonable?

*Miss Endicott slams the ledger shut causing Miss Laurelle to jump.
Daisy slides over and Miss Laurelle again has to push Daisy back
into place*

Miss Endicott Drink and drugs? No auditor would approve these
accounts. And you are all involved.
Mrs Bee I know nothing about auditors.
Miss Laurelle And I know nothing about accounts.
Miss Endicott (*pointing to Daisy*) You girl . . .
Mrs Hardie (*moving Daisy's head from side to side*) She knows
nothing about anything.
Miss Endicott This ledger reeks of mismanagement.
Mrs Bee We are handing out relief faster than reinforcements
arrive. Is that mismanagement? The needy mouth is an ever-
open door.
Miss Endicott For gin, rum and kummel? Where did it all go?
Poured into that ever-open mouth? I must have an answer.

Mrs Bee crosses to the cabinet and opens it

Mrs Bee Since you press me, dear Beatrice—most of it is before
you. Here. Not poured anywhere. Do you wish to take stock?
Miss Endicott A shameful exhibition.
Mrs Bee If a client cannot be tempted with gin, we have to try
kummel.

Miss Endicott Our clients are the *deserving* poor. Any so choosey cannot be deserving.

Mrs Bee Clients come in all shapes and sizes.

Miss Endicott Not our clients. (*Pointing to Daisy*) You, young lady. Have you been on the receiving end of this unbridled prodigality?

Mrs Hardie That's true enough.

Miss Endicott Well? Well?

Miss Laurelle (*twittering*) This situation is becoming impossible.

Mrs Bee Calm yourself. She won't give away any secrets.

Miss Endicott Won't she indeed? Are you one of those pampered parties with a predilection for high living. Eh? Eh?

Miss Laurelle No.

Miss Endicott I'm asking her.

Miss Laurelle I was answering for her.

Miss Endicott Can't she answer for herself?

Miss Laurelle I can't hold up much longer.

Mrs Bee Grit your teeth, Felicia, dear.

Miss Endicott Were you an accessory to fraud, girl? Have you been living a life of luxury on the contents of our collecting boxes? Lost your tongue? Dumb insolence. We can count that as a confession. Out with it, girl.

Miss Laurelle Oh. Oh. Oh!

Mrs Bee You have no right to bully her so, Beatrice.

Miss Endicott Speak!

Miss Laurelle Ooooh! (*She jumps up and retreats from Miss Endicott*)

Mrs Bee Silly Felicia.

Miss Endicott I'm speaking to you, girl, you!

Miss Endicott pokes Daisy with her cane. Daisy topples over and despite a last minute grab from Mrs Hardie, rolls off the couch

There is a pause

Mrs Hardie What now?

Mrs Bee Well?

Miss Endicott Not—dead?

Mrs Bee To the world.

Miss Endicott Disgusting.

Mrs Bee Remarkable the way she seems attracted to that particular spot.

Miss Endicott Were you aware of her condition?

Mrs Bee There are moments when honesty is not the best but the only policy. . . . Yes.

Miss Laurelle (*babbling*) I was not involved. And if I was, it was without my consent. And even if I did agree, what else could I have done? I deny it.

Miss Endicott Deny what?

Miss Laurelle Everything.

Mrs Hardie *We* didn't put her to sleep.

Miss Laurelle *We* didn't put gin in her tea.

Mrs Hardie Or laudenum in the gin.

Miss Endicott Who did?

Mrs Hardie (*turning to Mrs Bee*) Jane . . .

Miss Laurelle Dear Jane . . .

Mrs Bee How pleasant to know that one may rely on friends.

Mrs Hardie We do not make a practice of rendering innocent girls unconscious.

Miss Laurelle Or exporting them against their will.

Mrs Bee Let us be accurate. Technically speaking, not one of them was what you might call innocent. And some even enjoyed the sea air.

Miss Endicott Some? You mean more?

Mrs Bee Our customers have such varied tastes. A successful establishment must offer a wide selection.

Miss Endicott Of . . . of . . . ?

Mrs Bee I regard them as social workers. Very active in the fight against poverty. You are about to give utterance, Beatrice?

Miss Endicott This tea is cold.

Mrs Bee Let me pour fresh. No hot water. Dark brown and stiff with tannin.

Mrs Bee busies herself with pouring tea, in the course of which she unobtrusively tips the glass of kummel into the cup

Miss Endicott Do you expect me to take tea purchased from immoral earnings?

Mrs Bee Refreshments at these meetings have always been my personal contribution.

Miss Endicott (*grudgingly*) Small mercy.

Mrs Bee And I might add that, apart from an agreed percentage to the branch manager, not one penny from the Brussels end has been diverted from The Bequest.

Miss Endicott A judge may accept that plea in mitigation; but I advise you to engage a good lawyer. Soon.

Mrs Bee Our activities abroad are quite legal.

Miss Endicott Your activities here are not. It would pain me to see you all in custody.

Mrs Hardie It would pain us, too.

Miss Laurelle Yes, indeed.

Miss Endicott I see no alternative.

Mrs Bee There is always an alternative. When the bank advised me that our cupboard was bare there seemed no alternative to discontinuing our charity. Did I accept that "no alternative"? No. I won't bore you with details of how my idea came to me—on a tour of the Low Countries, as a matter of fact. It works—that is all you know, and all you need to know. ... Your tea, Beatrice. Any more for seed cake?

Miss Endicott (*taking her cup*) Now what is your alternative to arrest? With the evidence asleep at our feet. And Felicia and Maud as witnesses. How will the law view your idea?

Mrs Bee By the time the law arrives, the evidence will be on the high seas.

Miss Endicott Hah! (*She drinks*)

Mrs Bee Maud and Felicia will suffer lapses of memory.

Mrs Hardie You mean—lie?

Miss Laurelle Wouldn't that be perjury?

Mrs Bee Only when on oath. And this case will never reach a court. Will it, Maud? Will it, Felicia?

Miss Endicott This tea tastes of carraway.

Mrs Bee You've been eating seed cake. Too many seeds—remember?

Miss Endicott With an oddly aromatic quality. (*She finishes it*)

Mrs Bee It was stewed.

Miss Laurelle It was ...

Mrs Bee Yes, Felicia?

Mrs Hardie She drank it?

Mrs Bee (*taking the empty cup from Miss Endicott*) All.

Miss Endicott You must introduce me to your grocer—if you can spare the time before the prosecution. No, don't protest. On this point I cannot be moved. Principles must be maintained, if only for the instruction of the lower classes. Crime must be punished and abduction is a crime—no matter how worthy the cause. A martyr is sometimes a painful necessity, and your true martyr recognizes the fact. She goes down smiling. (*She yawns*)

Mrs Hardie This is like watching a battleship go down with all flags flying.

Miss Laurelle I've never seen a battleship go down. And I can't watch now.

Miss Endicott I'll visit you in prison. With words of comfort and instruction in the art of double-entry book-keeping. Our modern penal system offers splendid opportunities for further education. (*She yawns*)

Mrs Bee Do sit down, Beatrice.

Miss Endicott Sit? I feel about to fly.

Mrs Bee Over the sea?

Mrs Hardie What will she do there?

Mrs Bee As I pointed out, dear Maud, our clients are prepared to pay for a bizarre range of activities.

Miss Endicott (*swaying*) Where is my cane?

Mrs Bee Such opportunities for further education. In your hand, dear.

Miss Endicott My duty is clear. Smite the unrighteous.

Miss Endicott brings her cane down on the back of the couch. Miss Laurelle leaps up with a shriek

Mrs Hardie Was there enough laudenum?

Miss Endicott Smite them, I say.

Miss Endicott brings the cane down again. Miss Laurelle squeaks each time the cane hits the couch

Mrs Bee The usual dose.

Mrs Hardie Dear Beatrice never was usual.

Miss Endicott Again and again and again.

Miss Endicott continually brings the cane down on the back of the couch

Mrs Hardie Hush, dear. That's the tea talking.

Mrs Bee Restrain yourself, dear.

Miss Endicott Restrain?

Mrs Bee At least until you are installed on the other side. Nobody is paying for this expense of energy.

Miss Endicott I never felt so unrestrained.

Mrs Bee By this time Daisy was sleeping peacefully.
Mrs Hardie She still is.
Miss Endicott Down, you miserable offenders. Down. D. . . . (*She stops, sways and crumples*)
Miss Laurelle Oh. Now there are two. What shall we do? Oh!
Mrs Bee All you have to do, Felicia, is to behave as if nothing had happened.
Miss Laurelle I can't! I can't!
Mrs Bee Can't is a defeatist word.
Miss Laurelle I'll make a clean confession. I'll throw myself on the mercy of the court.
Mrs Bee Unwise, dear. It may throw you back into the cells.
Miss Laurelle (*hysterically*) I never dispensed soup. I never knitted comforts. I'll tell them I was seduced by Sunday School. Sunday School leads to Church. Church leads to charity. Charity leads to crime. I'll tell them I never went to Sunday School. I never learned the Ten Commandments. (*She begins to weep*)
Mrs Hardie Was brandy on your shopping list?
Mrs Bee Everything from cough-cure to quinine. (*She crosses to the cabinet and pours a glass of brandy*) I keep this for just such cases of cold feet.
Mrs Hardie Mustn't take too much notice of this outburst. Felicia can be trusted. You have to rely on our discretion now. After all, we all hang together.

Miss Laurelle wails even louder at the expression used by Mrs Hardie

Mrs Bee Brandy.
Mrs Hardie Thank you. (*She takes it and drinks it*)
Mrs Bee That was for Felicia.
Mrs Hardie Too bad. (*She hands the glass back*)
Mrs Bee Indeed. (*She fills another glass*) Can you be trusted with this one?
Mrs Hardie A little goes a long way.
Mrs Bee True.

Mrs Hardie takes the brandy and gives it to Miss Laurelle

Miss Laurelle Intoxicants are only for emergencies.
Mrs Hardie Shut your eyes and tell yourself it's castor oil. You'll feel much better afterwards.

Miss Laurelle If you insist. But I'll have no more to do with her. (*She drinks*)

Mrs Bee Perhaps the time has indeed come for me to move on. I'm inclined to transfer my abilities to a more restful location. Say Barchester.

Mrs Hardie Then I shan't recommend Barchester for a rest-cure.

Mrs Bee Moreover, philanthropy is finished. The rewards of self-denial are decidedly over-rated. Next time I set up an enterprise, it will be on my own account.

Mrs Hardie What's to become of this? Of—these. You can't leave them slumbering there.

Mrs Bee True. Before I retire, there are a few loose ends to be tied.

There is a knock at the door

Effie enters

Effie I've spoken to the carter, ma'am. He'll be round directly. To pick up the consignment for Harwich. One parcel.

Miss Laurelle One?

Mrs Hardie No, Effie. There are now two parcels.

Effie Is that so, ma'am? Two parcels?

Mrs Bee No, Effie. Four.

Mrs Hardie Four?

Mrs Bee Four.

Mrs Hardie and Miss Laurelle look at each other in sudden apprehension

Mrs Hardie
Miss Laurelle } (*together*) Four!

CURTAIN

FURNITURE AND PROPERTY LIST

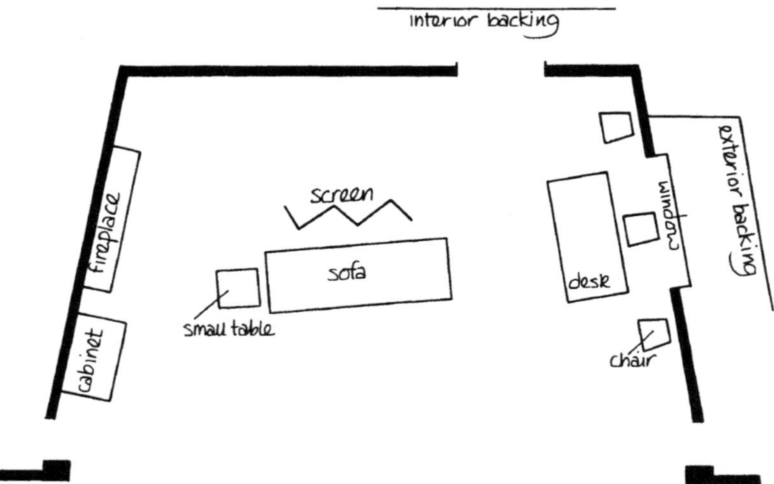

On stage: Fireplace. *In it:* vase of flowers
Cabinet. *In it:* assortment of bottles, decanters and glasses, box
    of sweets
Desk. *On it:* papers, ledger
3 chairs
Couch. *On it:* cushions
Low table
Screen
Assorted ornaments
Clock

Off stage: Tray with assortment of cups, saucers and plates, a seed cake
    (Effie)

Personal: **Mrs Bee:** purse and coins
Daisy: reticule
Miss Endicott: black cane

LIGHTING PLOT

Property fittings required: nil

To open: Full general lighting

No cues

EFFECTS PLOT

MADE AND PRINTED IN GREAT BRITAIN BY
LATIMER TREND & COMPANY LTD PLYMOUTH

MADE IN ENGLAND

www.ingramcontent.com/pod-product-compliance
Ingram Content Group UK Ltd.
Pitfield, Milton Keynes, MK11 3LW, UK
UKHW021820150726
7214IPUK00017B/234